Contents

Chapter 1 Bwark	7
Bonus: Map of the kingdom	20
Chapter 2 Earwigs and loo roll	23
Bonus: The castle	36
Chapter 3 Chicking	39
Bonus: Magatha's prank book	54
Chapter 4 Croneless	57
Bonus: Magatha and Garwick's top ten pranks	72
Chapter 5 The Great Prank War	75
Bonus: The battlefield	88
Chapter 6 Pranking the pranksters	91
Bonus: Trickmas	104
About the author	106
About the illustrator	108
Book chat	110

CHAPTER 1
Bwark

The king was a chicken, this much seemed certain. He hadn't always been a chicken. Until very recently, he'd been a perfectly normal king, with a crown, some ear hair, and a pair of those fancy pyjamas that said 'King' above the pocket in sticky-out lettering.

Now, however, he was a chicken. Or more accurately, a rooster. That's a boy chicken, in case you didn't know. He was about half a metre tall, covered in brown feathers, and had those scraggly red bits dangling off his head.

For a king, he made a fairly average looking chicken. There was nothing very regal about him as he sat at the dining table pecking the crumbs left over from the sandwich he'd just finished.

"Is he going to stay a chicken forever?" asked Magatha, the king's daughter, as she bent down to peer into her father's beady orange eyes.

"How should I know?!" barked Garwick, Magatha's twin brother. "You must have given him a hundred doses of the stuff!"

"No, I didn't!" shouted Magatha. "*You* did!"

The truth was, they were both a bit responsible. You see, Garwick and Magatha had been pranking each other for as long as they'd been alive. Longer, in fact. Like most twins, they had shared a womb, and they had pulled their first pranks before they'd even been born.

They weren't very good pranks, mind you. It's hard to prank someone in near total darkness when your brain's not fully developed. Mostly, it was just things like tapping the other twin on the shoulder, then pretending you hadn't. Stuff like that.

Anyway, it only got worse after they were born. Before they could even walk, the twins were pranking each other at every given opportunity. Plastic spiders in the baby milk. Whoopee cushions in the pram. Fart powder in the porridge.

As the years went on, most mornings, one or other of them would wake up to a toad in the bed or a bowl of custard over the door.

I tell you, it was exhausting for the poor king and queen. They were shattered!

"Please stop pranking one another!" the king had begged (back before he was a chicken).

"It's bound to end in tears!" the queen had predicted.

But did the twins listen? They did not! They just kept on pranking and pranking and pranking!

And as they grew older, their pranks grew ever more cunning. By the time they'd reached their tenth birthday, there was nothing Magatha and Garwick wouldn't do to get the better of one another.

They employed actors to be fake dentists, purchased dead snails by the truckload, and concocted home-made itching powders, invisible inks, foul-smelling perfumes and all manner of traps. Hour after hour was spent studying the most elaborate prank books they could lay their hands on. It was fair to say they were obsessed.

So, it was inevitable that, one day, one of them would stumble across the crone. Now, if you don't yet know about the mysterious figure rumoured to live out in the woods, it's about time you learned. To the townsfolk she was known simply as 'the crone'. No-one had met her in person, but everyone knew someone who had, or said they had, at least.

Here's a little rhyme to help you get better acquainted:

The crone lived alone, in a hovel of stone
far away from the throne, in the forested zone.
She was accident prone, though was not one to
  moan.
And at night, on her own, she would play
  the trombone.

That was a very silly rhyme. It didn't tell us any of the useful stuff, like how she spent most of her time making powerful potions, treacherous tonics and unimaginable ointments. Ones that could, for instance, turn a king into a chicken (if you're into that sort of thing).

Garwick and Magatha had heard tales of the crone since infancy. There were always rumours about her at court, but the twins had never been sure if the stories were true. In fact, if Garwick hadn't gone out riding with his horse, Dwayne, that morning, in search of fresh stinkberries, he might never have discovered her.

He'd paused for a moment by a particularly well-stocked stinkberry bush, when he noticed smoke rising from the undergrowth. As far as Garwick knew, no one lived out here in the depths of the forest. At first, he presumed someone must have made camp for the night. But then he noticed the hovel.

It wasn't the worst hovel he'd ever seen, nor was it the grandest. It was right in the middle. A five out of ten. No glass in the windows, but no holes in the roof either. And because there was no glass in the little building's window frames, Garwick had a clear view right into the heart of the place.

There, sitting on what appeared to be an unconscious goat, was an old, wizened woman. He decided it was only right to let himself in.

"Are you the crone?" asked Garwick, as he stepped inside the old woman's hovel.

"That I am," said the crone.

"Oh good," replied Garwick, looking about the old shamble-shack. "Rumour has it that you're skilled in the ways of potion making. Is this true?"

"'Tis true!" she replied. "I make potions and poisons and, occasionally, pancakes."

She held up a crusty black frying pan containing a rather sad looking pancake.

"Uh … no, thank you," said Garwick, politely. "I will, however, take one of your potions, please."

"Oh, will you now?" she replied with a tumble-toothed grin. "And just what sort of potion are you after?"

"Something that'll teach my sister a lesson, once and for all!"

"Once and for all?" she repeated, in a whisper. "I think I have just the thing!"

With that, she leaped up off the sleeping goat, sending pancake crumbs and toenail clippings hurtling across the room. She hurried over to where a crooked wooden cupboard sat nestled in the shadows and began to root around amongst the colourful bottles and jars within.

"No," she muttered, discarding a vial of sparkling purple gunk over one shoulder. "No," she repeated once more, tossing aside a pot of green glowing goop. "No," she grumbled a third time, chucking a test-tube of spiders' legs and vole dandruff into the fireplace.

"Ah!" she cried happily as she located the item she'd been hunting for. "Here it is! This is just the potion you'll be needing, young prince."

How odd, thought Garwick. He was sure he hadn't told her he was a prince.

"What does it do?" he asked, leaning in to examine the little glass bottle.

"What it does, it does well," she replied, with a grin. "To be sure, it is powerful. A drop should suffice."

"Right, yes, just a drop," said Garwick, reaching for the potion. "And what exactly will it cost me?"

To this, the crone only smiled.

CHAPTER 2

Earwigs and loo roll

Unlike her rotten, no-good brother, who was no doubt off hunting for stinkberries again, Magatha had stayed back at the castle that morning to hatch plans of her own. It could be tough coming up with new pranks after so many years spent trying to outsmart one another. Sometimes, you just had to take the time to sit and think up some fresh ideas.

Magatha couldn't count the number of times she'd hidden ripe cheese inside Garwick's mattress or glued his shoes to the floor. Slipping a drop of squid ink inside her brother's face wash was always a delight.

She never got tired of seeing him arrive at the breakfast table with bright blue cheeks. And though she still enjoyed these classics, some days, Magatha just wanted to pull a prank she'd never pulled before.

Magatha took a seat in her favourite thinking spot, at the very top of the castle's north tower. The view from the roof was spectacular. All the way from Frogspawn Forest, down to the Marshes of Malcolm, and right across to the vast and foreboding Ostrich Bone Graveyard.

It was a great place to ponder, plot and prepare. Also, you could drop things on people from up here if you wanted to, but Magatha felt quite cheerful today, so she wasn't in the mood for that. She pulled out her hand-made compendium of pranks – a great big leatherbound book, bursting with every single prank she'd ever dreamed up – and opened it to a blank page.

"OK, Mags, time to think," she said to herself. "How shall we ruin Garwick's day?"

The first thing she scribbled at the top was: *Earwigs in ears.*

But it sounded too much like a torture and not enough like a prank, so she scribbled it out.

Next, she wrote: *Frozen loo roll (cold bum).*

But after ten minutes of thinking, she couldn't figure out a way to keep a loo roll chilled long enough to freeze her brother's bottom. Again, she scribbled it out.

After a long time thinking, she eventually wrote down the word: *Toothpaste*…

It felt like a good start – but it wasn't quite enough. She had a strange feeling she might be onto something though. The question was what? Would she do something to his toothpaste? To his toothbrush? To his teeth? She couldn't quite figure it out.

"Magatha!" came a sudden voice that made her jump.

"Oh, hello, Dad," she replied, turning to see her father leaning out of one of the tower's windows.

"I've told you about climbing around up here!" he grumbled. "You'll fall to your death one of these days, and do you know who'll be to blame?"

"Garwick?" suggested Magatha.

"No, not Garwick – YOU!" snapped her dad, before adding: "And also possibly Garwick, yes. I wouldn't put it past him. He'd definitely be questioned anyway."

"Don't worry, Dad," said Magatha, with a giggle. "He doesn't want to do me in. That would spoil his fun. And mine."

"When are you two going to grow out of all this prank business?" asked the king, sounding bored to tears with it all. "Aren't you old enough to call it a day?"

"Perhaps tomorrow," said Magatha, grinning. "Today, I think I'm onto something."

The king shook his head and went back inside, closing the window behind him. When Magatha looked down at her page again, she found she'd let her pen wobble its way across the paper unchecked. It had left a squiggle of ink in its path.

She stared at it, squinted, and drew the page closer. It almost – not quite, but almost – looked like a word scribbled there right beside 'toothpaste'. But what did it say? Sardine? Sasquatch? Sandpit?

"Sandwich!" she cried, when the word suddenly became clear to her. "Toothpaste sandwich! That's it!"

She'd never made a toothpaste sandwich before! Not in all her years of pranking! She couldn't help but smile. The idea, Magatha felt, had all the hallmarks of a classic trick. It was simple, annoying, gross, non-lethal.

And what made it all the better was the knowledge of just how much Garwick hated brushing his teeth. It was perfect!

With her conundrum solved, she clambered back through the window and into the tower, then tore off in the direction of her bedroom. Just as Magatha rounded the corner that led to her door, she ran straight into Garwick with a crash. The pair fell over backwards, each letting out a great yell.

"Garwick!" cried Magatha, sitting up. "What are you doing down here? This corridor leads only to my room!"

It was true, there was only one more door down the corridor and it was the door to her bedroom. Magatha had a strong (and perfectly reasonable) suspicion that her brother had been up to no good.

"I was looking for you," replied Garwick, innocently.

"Oh really? What for?"

"I – " began Garwick, then faltered. "Uh ... I've forgotten. But it was a perfectly normal reason and not remotely suspicious."

"Stay out of my room!" she growled, storming past him and slamming the door behind her.

Once inside the room, Magatha looked around to see what Garwick might have done. Nothing looked different, at a glance. She checked the bed for raw eggs. She checked her sock drawer for stinkbugs. She checked her wardrobe for live squirrels (it wouldn't be the first time). But there was nothing.

Deciding it was safe, Magatha grabbed her tube of toothpaste and slipped it into the pocket of her dress. When she peered out of the door, Garwick was nowhere to be seen. Magatha hurried out into the hallway, down the corridor and out onto the stairwell that led down to the kitchens.

The royal cook, Parfred Bunderbeek, was a grumpy man at the best of times. His face was as red as a boiled lobster and he was always furious. He shouted at his staff, at the guards and at the castle's cats, rats and bats. It took all his self-control not to shout at the royal family whenever they spoke to him. But boy could he cook, so no one really minded.

"All right, Bunderbeek," said Magatha, cheerfully. "I'm after some bread."

"I don't have any," growled Parfred Bunderbeek, who was busy stirring a great steaming vat of what appeared to be crows.

"Yes, you do," said Magatha. "There's a ton of bread just there."

She was right, there was lots of bread right beside him.

"That's not for you," he snapped. "That's for lunch."

"I need it for lunch," countered Magatha.

"You're not the cook!" he barked.

"I am today," she replied, with a grin, and snatched a loaf from the counter.

"Oi!" yelled the furious cook, whipping out his ladle so fast he sprayed crow juice right across the ceiling.

But it was too late! Giggling, Magatha was already gone, heading off in the direction of the grand dining hall. It was almost lunchtime and toothpaste sandwiches were on the menu …

THE CASTLE

CHAPTER 3
Chicking

Garwick was grinning. Magatha was grinning. The kitchen boy, Barry, was grinning (but that's because he'd farted and no one had noticed).

The king was ignoring the lot of them, and was already tucking into his lunch at the head of the table. The queen was yet to appear. She'd been off somewhere all morning, getting up to whatever queens get up to when they're not sitting on thrones and the likes. Perhaps water-skiing?

"How are you feeling?" asked Garwick, studying his sister.

"Fine, thanks," she replied. "How's your lunch?"

Garwick looked down at the sandwich on his plate.

"You know, I've not tried it yet," he said, innocently, before reaching to lift it up.

"Do enjoy," said Magatha, trying her best not to seem overly interested.

Garwick was just about to take a bite when he lowered the sandwich once again and asked: "Are you *sure* you're feeling OK, dear sister?"

"Why shouldn't I be?" asked Magatha, starting to sound suspicious.

"No reason, no reason at all," he replied, and took a large bite of his sandwich.

Magatha's grin grew even bigger as she watched him chew. Ha! Any second he'd …

"Mmm! Delicious!" announced Garwick.

"What?!" spluttered Magatha.

"What do you mean, '*what*'?" asked Garwick, peering at her over the bite mark in his bread.

"Does it taste OK?" she enquired. "Your sandwich?"

"It tastes delicious," he replied. "Best sandwich I've ever had. How about yours, *Dad*?"

"Bwark," came the unexpected reply from the king.

Both twins turned to look. There, in their father's seat, sat a great brown rooster.

"Oh goodness!" said Magatha.

"What have you done?" cried Garwick.

"What have *I* done?" shouted Magatha. "What have *you* done!?"

"Guards! Off with her head!" yelled Garwick, to no one in particular. Barry, the farting kitchen boy, had left now and they were alone.

"*My* head?" squawked Magatha. "I haven't done anything!"

"You turned Dad into a chicken!" snapped Garwick.

"No, I didn't!"

"You must have! What did you put in his sandwich?"

"I didn't touch his sandwich!"

"OK, then what did you put in *my* sandwich?" yelled Garwick.

"Toothpaste!" cried Magatha. "Why? Did you swap sandwiches?!"

Garwick was quiet now. He was beginning to grow quite pale. "Toothpaste?" he murmured. "Whose toothpaste?"

"Mine, of course," said Magatha. "Why?"

"Ah ... well – " replied Garwick. "That explains it then."

"Have you done something to my toothpaste?" Magatha hissed.

"Well ... I may have ... *meddled with it.*"

"Meddled with it? MEDDLED WITH IT? Dad is a chicken, Garwick! What did you do!?"

Garwick let out a sigh. This was going to take some explaining.

"You know all those stories about the crone in the woods?" he began.

"Mm-hm," replied Magatha, fixing her brother with a hard stare.

"Well, it turns out they're true. I found her. She's … odd."

"She's *odd*? And you thought it was a good idea to buy some magic chicken potion from her and stick it in Dad's sandwich, did you?"

"Firstly, I didn't know it was chicken potion," said Garwick, defensively. "And secondly, I didn't put it in his sandwich, I put it in *your* toothpaste!"

"But I put *my* toothpaste in *your* sandwich!" cried Magatha.

"Well, I swapped *my* sandwich with *Dad's*!"

"Why on earth would you do that?!" she yelled, throwing her hands up.

"Because I had a feeling you were tricking me! It's not often you prepare lunch for us, you know!"

"Oh, for crying out – " she spluttered. "This is all your fault!"

"*My* fault?!" yelled Garwick. "*You're* the one who filled my sandwich with toothpaste!"

"And you're the one who mixed my toothpaste with chicken potion!"

"If I'd known you'd made me a toothpaste sandwich, I'd have never given it to Dad!"

"And if I'd known you'd meddled with my toothpaste, I'd have thrown it in the moat!"

"I was only meant to give you a tiny little bit," said Garwick, looking glum. "That's why I chose toothpaste. People only ever use a tiny bit of toothpaste."

"Unless they're making a toothpaste sandwich," replied Magatha, sounding equally glum.

The dining hall was terribly silent for a time.

"Bwark," said the king.

"What are we going to do now?" asked Garwick.

"We'll have to tell Mum," replied Magatha.

"Really? Do we have to?" groaned Garwick.

This was just the sort of thing the queen wasn't going to take well. She always struggled to see the funny side of the children's pranks. She'd been livid the time Magatha had dyed Garwick's eyebrows while he slept. And even more furious the following day when Garwick had floated Magatha's bed out onto the lake (while she was still in it, sleeping). And she'd still never quite forgiven either of them for the city-wide food fight they'd caused during the king's jubilee celebrations.

So you can imagine why they felt a little apprehensive about their mother finding out they'd turned her husband into a chicken. Turns out, they wouldn't have to worry for long…

"Garrrrgggghhh!" screeched the queen, who'd entered the room unnoticed a moment earlier. "There's a chicken on the table!"

"Technically, it's a rooster," said Garwick.

"Technically, it's the king," added Magatha.

"What?" spluttered the queen. "What's that supposed to mean? Where's your father?"

"That's what we're trying to tell you, Mum," said Garwick. "He's on the table. He's a chicken."

"Rooster," corrected Magatha.

The queen looked from one to the other, then over at the chicken. "I see," she said and, without taking her eyes off the chicken, called for the guards.

What followed could best be described as chaos. The guards fetched the royal doctor. The royal doctor called the royal advisers. The royal advisers fetched the greatest chicken experts in the kingdom. The dining hall soon filled up with a great throng of panicked professionals doing their best to resolve a situation they had no idea how to fix.

The king pottered about finishing off a second sandwich (peanut butter and marmalade, this time). Garwick and Magatha stood to one side, quietly debating which of them was *most* in the wrong. The queen looked on, wide-eyed at the chaos.

"It's clearly you, Garwick," explained Magatha. "You crossed a line with this whole crone business."

"Oh really? You'd have done it too, if you'd thought of it!" snapped Garwick.

It was true. Magatha had long dreamed of exploiting the crone's magical pranking powers. She'd just never been fortunate enough to stumble across the hovel herself.

"I most certainly wouldn't have!" declared Magatha, offended.

"Don't be ridiculous! You'd have made the same choice I did, if you'd found her!"

"Where did you find her?" asked Magatha. "Do you think you could find her again?"

"Sure. I know exactly where she is. Why?"

"Why do you think!? Dad's a chicken!"

"A rooster."

"Whatever! If anyone can turn him back, it's the crone!"

"Right," said Garwick. "Do you want me to draw you a map, then?"

"You're coming too! This is *your* fault!"

"*Our* fault," he corrected her.

"Whatever, just get your coat!"

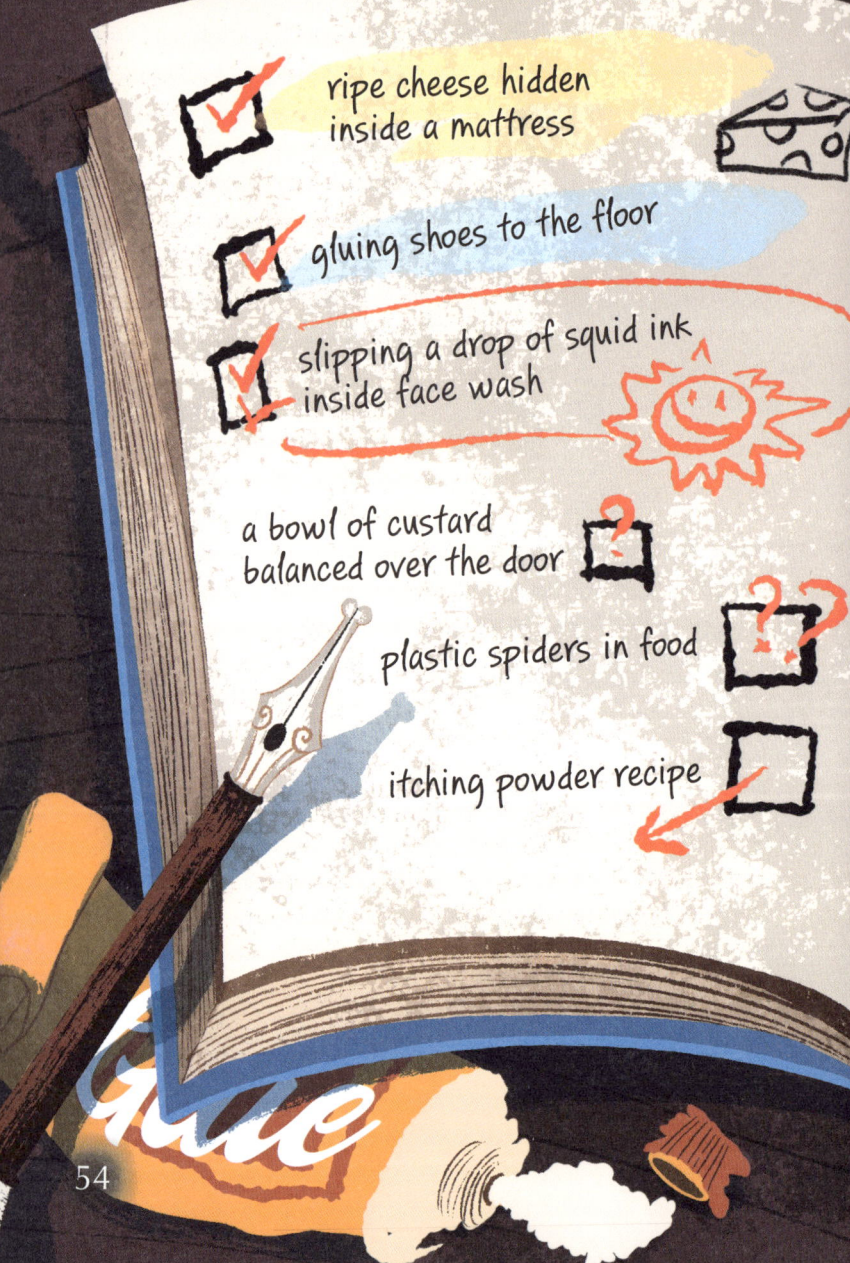

CHAPTER 4
Croneless

It would have been quicker getting back to the crone's clearing, if the twins had just laid off the pranking for a bit. But do you think they managed a truce? Of course they didn't. Garwick had barely got his boots on when he fell head over heels into a broom cupboard.

"Magatha!" he yelled, realising his bootlaces had been tied together. "This is hardly the time!"

"Sorry," replied Magatha, her smile vanishing as she discovered *someone* had sewn her coat sleeve shut at the elbow.

Now it was Garwick's turn to be amused. "I forgot I'd done that," he added, sounding pleased with himself. "Oh, and you might find a few pine cones in your – "

"Ow," said Magatha, discovering the pine cones in her shoes a moment too late. "Very funny."

"Thank you," he replied, bowing.

"Almost as funny as the custard I left in your hat," she added, cheerfully.

Custard was already dripping down Garwick's ears by the time he realised what she'd done. "Sometimes, dear sister, I really don't like you."

"Nor I you, dearest brother," she replied, and together they headed out into the afternoon sunshine.

A few hours later, as they marched through the woods, the twins were no longer speaking. Since leaving the castle, Garwick had stepped on the heel of Magatha's shoe 36 times, causing it to fall off and send her stumbling.

Magatha, for her part, took quiet satisfaction in the growing swarm of wasps trailing her brother, thanks to the super-sticky pipple-fruit seeds she'd stuck to his back.

"Get off!" yelled Garwick, swinging his fists around in an unsuccessful attempt at punching the irritating insects. "Just leave me alone!"

"They seem to like you, don't they?" said Magatha, innocently, as she paused to rub the blister forming on her heel.

"This is your doing," growled Garwick. "I thought we were going to stop pranking each other until we fixed Dad."

"What do you call stepping on the back of my shoe, then?" said Magatha, crossing her arms.

"That's not a prank!" argued Garwick. "That's just me annoying you for fun."

"Well, sticking pipple-fruit seeds to your back is just *my* way of annoying *you* for fun!" she replied.

"You're impossible," he snapped, then stormed away in a cloud of wasps.

For a moment, Magatha felt like letting him go off by himself. They'd been looking for the crone's hovel for hours now. She'd probably find it faster on her own. But then she'd have no one to annoy on the walk home, and what fun was that?

So she hurried off after him.

Another two hours and there was still no sign of the crone, her hovel, or any hint of a ceasefire between the twins.

Magatha was now dripping with mud from where Garwick had tricked her into stepping into a swamp. And Garwick was still hiccupping after he'd unwittingly accepted one of the sweets Magatha was eating. Turns out the blue ones his sister had been avoiding were filled with chilli powder.

By this point, two things were starting to grow clear to the twins. Firstly, no matter how much they might want to, they just couldn't stop pranking one another. And secondly, the crone's hovel was *not* where Garwick thought it was.

"I swear, it was right here!" he cried. "Look, those are the stinkberry bushes I told you about!"

"Hmm," said Magatha, examining the nearby thicket. "Someone's been at these, for sure."

"Yes!" said Garwick. "Me! I was picking them to put in your porridge when I spotted the smoke. That's when I saw the hovel. Right over there in that clearing!"

But now the clearing stood entirely empty. No stone hovel. No crone. No sign that anyone had been there.

"It's magic!" declared Garwick.

"Well, obviously," said Magatha. "A magic old woman does something magical. It's not that unexpected."

"I wasn't expecting it!"

"That's because you're as thick as a castle wall."

"And you're as dense as a dungeon door."

"You're as slow as a cart without wheels."

"And you're as dim as a cave without candles."

This went on for another 23 minutes, until they'd exhausted every possible comparison for each other's idiocy.

"You're as – " began Garwick, then paused for a bit. "I can't think of any more."

"Me neither," said Magatha. "Shall we go home?"

"OK then," replied Garwick.

And with that, they set off in the direction of the castle. Neither spoke a word. They were so busy dreading the consequences awaiting them, they forgot to prank each other the entire way home.

"The king is still a chicken!" announced one of the royal advisers, as the twins walked into the throne room.

"It's all Garwick's fault," said Magatha, before her brother could get a word in.

"*You're* the one who put the potion in the sandwich!" snapped Garwick.

"And *you* put it in the toothpaste!" yelled Magatha.

"SHUSH!" yelled the queen. "It doesn't matter which of you put what where," she continued. "The fact is, you're both to blame. You and this endless prank war of yours!"

"Sorry, Mum," said Magatha.

"Sorry, Mum," said Garwick.

"What am I meant to do with sorries?" snapped the queen. "Sorries won't turn your father back to normal! Sorries won't rule the kingdom! Sorries won't get the chicken droppings out of my lace tablecloth!"

"Perhaps some bleach?" suggested one of the advisers.

"Quiet, Ugmond!" snapped the queen. "What we need, above all, is a new ruler. So, who's it to be, hmm?"

There was silence. Everyone looked at everyone else.

"Bwark," said the king, who was sitting upon his throne, pecking at a pretzel.

"Surely it's got to be you, Mum?" said Garwick. "You're the queen. You know what you're doing better than anyone."

"I can't rule the kingdom! I have no royal blood in me," she snapped. "You'd know that if you spent less time thinking up pranks and more time studying the rules of succession. There are only three living individuals with a claim to the throne, and one of them is a chicken."

"Rooster," corrected Ugmond the adviser.

"Oh, be quiet," snapped the queen.

"So you're saying – " began Garwick, "one of *us* has to take over from Dad?"

"That's right," replied the queen. "Your father had always hoped you would rule together. What do you say?"

There was silence as the twins looked at one another. Then at the royal advisers. Then at the chicken that had once been king.

"Gulp," said Garwick.

"You don't say 'gulp'," replied Magatha, rolling her eyes. "You just swallow. Loudly. No one actually *says* 'gulp'."

"I do!" snapped Garwick. "I like saying 'gulp'. Gulp!"

"You're as simple as a one-piece jigsaw," said Magatha (who'd thought up an extra one on the walk home).

"Yeah? I'd still make a better king than you!" shouted Garwick.

"And I'd make a better *queen* than you!" yelled Magatha.

And with that, the Great Prank War had begun …

MAGATHA AND GARWICK'S TOP TEN PRANKS

10. Tricking someone into stepping into a swamp.

9. Hiding pine cones in shoes.

8. Stepping on someone's heels as they walk.

7. Pouring custard into a hat.

6. Tying bootlaces together.

5. Putting stinkberries in porridge.

4. Sewing coat sleeves closed at the elbow.

3. Sticking fruit seeds to the back of someone's coat.

2. Offering hiccupping sweets (blue works well).

1. Dishing out a toothpaste sandwich.

CHAPTER 5
The Great Prank War

The kingdom was divided. Queen Magatha or King Garwick. Which would it be?

"*She* should be queen!" argued an old man over dinner that night. "She's the eldest!"

"Only by 11 seconds!" barked his wife. "But the boy's a boy! That's what counts! It's tradition!"

"It's old-fashioned!"

"No, it isn't!"

"Yes, it is!"

"No, it's not!"

"Is!"

"Not!"

"Is!"

"Not!" etc, etc, etc ...

Arguments like that were taking place in every home, in every county of the kingdom. Wives were turning on husbands, brothers on sisters, kids on their parents, and even cats upon dogs (though they were already enemies, so no one noticed).

And just how does one settle such a particular pickle of a problem? Why, you follow the example set by your would-be rulers. You prank! And boy, did the people prank. It started small, of course ...

One wife gave up arguing with her husband and simply poured a great mountain of salt into her pot of nettle and goat-hoof stew. She fell about laughing as he swallowed a great mouthful of the eye-watering slop.

The husband pouted and said, "Tastes better for it, anyway!" and decided that he would fill his wife's shoes with jelly when she wasn't looking.

Pretty soon, the whole kingdom was in the throes of a prank Armageddon: ringing each other's doorbells and running off, sending midnight pizzas to one another's homes, leaving buckets of water over their neighbour's doorframes … And, as is always the case with pranks, this only led to retaliation, and that led to escalation.

Before long, groups of pranksters were going from town to town, armed with fart gas and plastic vomit, all in the name of their preferred monarch. Team Magatha or Team Garwick. Everyone picked a side.

First, the people got angry, then they got organised, then they got creative. The Great Prank War was in full swing within the week. Legendary mischief unfolded across the land: the Night of a Thousand Whoopee Cushions, the Great Itching Powder Plot, the Stink Bomb Siege of Saddlewick. Brilliant and horrifying in equal measure.

Never in history had so many people woken up so itchy. Never before had sneezing powder been deployed by catapult. There was so much fake dog poo laid across the no-man's land between Gruckford Quarry and Pimpleton, that no one dared cross it in anything less than the sturdiest of welly boots.

The cost to the kingdom was astronomical. Everyone was too busy pranking to do any work. No one made anything or paid any taxes. Crops failed as farmers stayed up all night drawing fake moustaches on each other's sleeping faces.

An enormous rise in the use of cheques signed with disappearing ink led to the closure of half a dozen major banks. In short, unless you were lucky enough to own a joke shop, you were in trouble.

It's said that the Great Prank War reached its peak on the third and final day of the Battle of Bumford Moor. For 48 hours straight, armies of pranksters, loyal to Queen Magatha and King Garwick, had faced each other. They had hurled every trick, trap, gag and ploy in existence across the soggy, custard-splattered battlefield. They had fought through mud and jelly, across barricades made of upside-down furniture, and under skies darkened by paint balloons and glitter cannons. The battlefield was a mess. A stinking, gloopy, glittery mess. Banana skins carpeted the ridges.

Both armies had called for a ceasefire earlier that afternoon so they could sit down and eat jam sandwiches. But even that had ended badly, when someone had replaced all Garwick's rations with drawings of food.

Magatha stood before her troops, crown askew, her sceptre now just a stick with a rubber chicken on the end.

"This has all got a bit out of hand, hasn't it?" she said to her second-in-command.

"Your Highness," replied Dame Finika Craggsnattle, who was holding a live goose under one arm and a cream pie in the other. "I must confess ... I have no idea what's going on anymore."

Magatha stared out over the moor. Somewhere, off in the mist, someone blew a haunting kazoo. Across the field, in his command tent, Garwick was studying his battlefield plans.

"We have itchy soldiers, sneezing horses and someone's gone and painted inappropriate images on every flag," reported Sir Arbut Nullwick, Garwick's Chief Prank Marshal.

"What am I doing?" muttered Garwick.

"Waging the silliest war in history, I believe," replied Nullwick. "And we shall be victorious! Of that I have no doubt."

"But at what cost?" said Garwick, softly.

The air was thick with tension – and a suspicious smell of boiled cabbage – as Magatha and Garwick began their steady march towards one another across the moor. They met in the middle of no-man's land, ankle-deep in jelly.

"All right," said Garwick. "What do you say we call this one a draw?"

"Fine," agreed Magatha. "But only if you admit I would've won."

"I'd rather wear exploding trousers for the rest of my life," Garwick snorted.

"That can be arranged," said Magatha, grinning.

There was a long pause. In the distance, a lone whoopee cushion sounded mournfully in the breeze.

"We've ruined the kingdom, haven't we?" said Garwick, at last.

"A little bit, yeah," admitted Magatha.

They turned and looked back at their armies: tired pranksters slumped in banana-peel trenches, exhausted fart bombers cleaning custard off their helmets, prank pigeons circling overhead in confused loops.

"I'm sorry," said Garwick. "For going to the crone. For Dad. For everything."

"Me too," said Magatha. "I shouldn't have made that sandwich."

"And I shouldn't have meddled with your toothpaste."

"We're both to blame."

"Agreed."

They offered each other a sticky handshake. The moment their hands touched, a small spark crackled between them. Neither had remembered to remove their joy buzzers. They chuckled as they discarded them in the mud.

"Draw?" said Magatha.

"Draw," agreed Garwick.

And with that, the Great Prank War was at an end.

A strange quiet fell across the moor. Both armies watched, confused, as their leaders turned and walked away from the centre of the field.

"So ... now what?" Garwick asked.

"I guess we go and apologise to Mum. Try to fix the kingdom. Somehow."

But before they could take another step ...

"PFFFFFT!"

An enormous whoopee cushion let loose from beneath their feet. With a terrible quacking parp, a noxious gas cloud filled the air. It swirled around the twins, causing them to cough and splutter. From somewhere within the stinking mist, there came a shrill, mocking laugh. The children were terrified. As the fog began to clear, they could make out the shape of an elderly figure, hunched and dark.

"Who's there?" asked Garwick.

"Don't you remember me, boy?" she replied.

"Crone?" whispered Garwick.

"Mum?" gasped Magatha.

The figure in the haze lifted off her wig and smiled at them.

"Hello, children," said the queen. "You didn't think I'd let this nonsense go on forever, did you?"

CHAPTER 6

Pranking the pranksters

Have you ever heard the sound of two enormous armies bursting into laughter at the same time? It's astonishing. A great tsunami of chuckles crashing against your eardrums. Between the thunderous roar and the shock of their mother appearing out of nowhere, the twins turned pale as parchment.

"I ... I don't – " stammered Garwick. "You can't be her?"

"A little bit of make-up, a change of wardrobe," replied the queen, grinning.

"You mean you were the crone all along!?" spluttered Magatha.

"More than that, dear. I invented her. The whole story." The queen gave a small bow.

The twins just stared at their mother, open-mouthed. What in the world was going on?

"I started the legend years ago," she continued. "Just a little bedtime story, at first. A way to keep you from wandering too far into the woods when you were small. But thanks to the pair of you chattering away to anyone who'd listen, the story soon spread. I forgot all about it until recently, when my old friend the crone turned out to be useful again. Only this time round, I decided to play her myself."

"But … the potion!" said Garwick.

"And Dad!" added Magatha.

The queen smiled a cunning smile. "Perhaps now would be a good time to turn around."

The twins turned slowly to look behind them. And there he was. The king. Very much not a chicken. Very much alive. He was holding an actual chicken under one arm like a handbag.

"Hello, children," he said, cheerfully. "Miss me?"

Magatha nearly fell over.

"But ... I saw you change!" cried Garwick.

"Are you quite sure?" asked the queen. "Were you *actually* looking at him when it happened?"

Garwick frowned. "Well ... no. I didn't exactly see him *change*. I was looking at Magatha."

"And I was looking at Garwick," said Magatha. "But one minute you were there, and the next – "

"And the next, I was under the table," said the king, stroking the chicken affectionately. "This is Brian, by the way. Bit of a grump when he hasn't eaten."

"Bwark," said Brian, who was starting to get hungry.

The twins turned back to their mother.

"So you … *pranked* us?!" said Magatha, still barely able to believe it.

"We did," replied the queen. "All of us."

And as she said it, the two great armies exploded into cheering and laughter.

"They knew?" gasped Garwick. "*ALL* of them?"

"Not at first," replied the queen. "It took a good while to get the word out that your father wasn't *really* a chicken. But yes, eventually, everyone knew."

"And they all played along," added the king. "Pranking the pranksters."

"But what about the hovel?" said Garwick. "When we got back there, it was gone!"

"Built in a day by the royal carpenter," replied the queen. "Then packed up by sunset."

"And the potion?" asked Magatha.

"Mint sauce. Bit of glitter. Harmless," said the king.

"Why!?" cried Garwick. "Why would you do this to us?"

"You two really are quite incredible," said the queen. "You're creative. Clever. Cunning."

"And completely out of control," added the king. "We wanted you to rule side by side one day. But to do that, you had to learn to work together. Otherwise, you would have torn the kingdom apart."

"As you've demonstrated," said the queen, with a piercing look.

"We've ruined everything, haven't we?" mumbled Garwick, looking out across the mucky battleground at his squalid troops.

"It's nothing we can't set right. When the two of you put your heads together, there's little you can't achieve," said the queen.

The twins' armies had begun to gather to watch this historic moment unfold. Some were still holding pies. A few had buckets full of custard. They were murmuring to one another. Wondering if this was all over at last.

The queen raised a hand, and the entire crowd went silent. "I want every last one of you to go home," she called out. "The Great Prank War is at an end. You've all done brilliantly. Now go and do your actual jobs."

And with a great cheer, the crowd began to disperse. Townsfolk and soldiers trudged off, trailing streamers and silly string behind them.

Garwick and Magatha stood side by side, watching it all melt away.

"I can't believe we fell for it," said Garwick.

"I can," said Magatha. "We always fall for it."

"We do?"

"Over the years, you've pranked me eleven-thousand-three-hundred-and-forty-two times," said Magatha.

"Have I?" asked Garwick, sounding both astonished and rather pleased with himself.

"I kept notes," explained Magatha. "But do you know how many of them I've fallen for?"

"No," replied Garwick.

"All but two," she said, with a smile. "You really are the greatest prankster I've ever met."

"Well, y*ou're* the greatest prankster *I've* ever met," he told her, with a grin of his own.

"Maybe it's time we started working together?" suggested Magatha.

"I'm game if you are," replied Garwick.

"Bwark," added Brian – who had played his part to perfection.

From that day forth, the twins worked together hand in hand (not literally of course, that would be impractical and a bit odd). They spent weeks helping to clean up the kingdom and put right the chaos they had caused.

They organised squads of soldiers to sweep away the custard and jelly that filled the gutters and clogged the drains. They personally oversaw the great 'de-pooing' of no-man's land, removing over seven tonnes of plastic dog waste. They worked without a break or prank, until the job was done. Mum and Dad were very proud.

The king went on to live a long, full life, and the queen an even longer, fuller one. When Garwick and Magatha eventually took the throne, many years later, they did so together. They ruled wisely and well for the rest of their days, over a kingdom that loved them as much as a kingdom had ever loved anything (ice cream and theme parks and waterslides included).

And if you're wondering whether they stopped their pranking entirely, I'm pleased to report that they did. Well ... almost.

It was set by royal decree that, for just one day a year, everyone in the kingdom was free to prank anyone else without fear of punishment or reprisal. The lowliest of farmhands could, for instance, make a cowpat pie for King Garwick and not get into a jot of trouble. The meekest of maids could fill Queen Magatha's slippers with slugs and face no consequences other than a pat on the back and a warm "you got me," from Her Majesty.

Trickmas, as it became known, was soon the kingdom's favourite holiday, enjoyed by young and old, rich and poor, chicken and rooster. And each year, as the sun set on a long day's pranking, every family in the land would settle down to enjoy a traditional Trickmas delicacy: an enormous platter of the finest Toothpaste Sandwiches.

TRICKMAS

About the author

What made you want to be an author?

I always loved making stuff up and making people laugh. I'm dyslexic and found lots of things about school quite tough. But writing, once I could do it on a laptop (which made it faster and neater) was always a pleasure. I couldn't see myself doing anything else.

Henry White

How did you come up with the idea for this book?

Well, I was eating my breakfast toothpaste sandwich when I … No, not really. I've never eaten a toothpaste sandwich in my life. But there's something a bit funny about toothpaste. Even the word. And I always like the idea of using something for a purpose it's not intended. Like a flamingo to play golf.

What's your favourite type of book to write?

Definitely something funny. And kids love funny, so a funny book for kids is as good as it gets. I also like sci-fi and horror and stuff like that, which you can actually mix in with comedy really well. So a daft science-fiction story for kids is right up my street.

Where do you like to write?

I like to get out of the house and write where there are lots of people about, so I often go to a café. After a while, wherever I live, I find a spot with a favourite comfy chair, a nice view out of the window and, ideally, nice coffee and pastries. Then I write.

Do you have a favourite part of this book?
I like some of the silliness in the prank war. And the mournful whoopee cushion farting into the breeze.

What do you hope readers will get from this book?
Ideas for how to prank responsibly …

Do you think the twins will continue to prank each other?
I think that once the twins have recognised that there's a time and a place for pranking, they'll only prank each other occasionally, rather than letting it dominate their whole lives. But yes, they'll be pranking each other all the way to the grave.

What do you want your next book to be about?
I've no idea. Maybe something about a dog who yawns so wide, he swallows his own head and ends up in another dimension.

What was your favourite book when you were a kid?
When I was young, I remember my dad reading *Matilda* to me and loving it (even though he kept dozing off while he was reading). I think the mix of humour, mischief and comedy was right up my street. There's still no one quite like Roald Dahl.

What would you do at Trickmas?
I'd make my kids think they were going somewhere really awful, somewhere they just dreaded. "Come on, kids, time to get your vaccinations again!" I'd tell them. But really, I'd take them somewhere brilliant, like Disneyland or a chocolate factory. Pranks can be nice too.

About the illustrator

Did you always want to be an illustrator?

Actually, I studied architecture at university. I earned my bachelor's degree in architecture, and for a while, I thought I would be an architect.

How did you get into illustrating?

I've always loved reading books, especially the ones with pictures.

Mai Ngo

As a kid, I could spend hours with paper, pencils, and crayons, drawing all the stories I adored. Later, while studying architecture, illustration turned into my little side job. One day, I received a commission to work on a picture book series, and it instantly brought back my childhood dreams. The more I explored picture books and visual storytelling, the more I realised that being an illustrator is truly my biggest passion.

What was the most challenging thing about illustrating this book?

I love stories with a good sense of humour. Of course, humour comes in many forms: gentle, dark, and everything in between. The tricky part was creating illustrations that not only make kids laugh but also feel right for their age.

Do you use pens and paints or do you work digitally?
Watercolour is my favourite medium. I use watercolour and pencil sketches during the concept stage of every project.

What was your favourite scene to illustrate?
My favourite was the scene where Garwick and Magatha watch their war melt away.

Which character in the book did you identify with the most?
Definitely Magatha!

Which character was the most fun to draw?
The Crone, aka the Queen.

Have you ever pranked someone in real life?
Oh, yes! My younger brother. We're only 18 months apart in age, so we practically grew up like twins. When we were kids, we never got tired of pranking each other. We did things like sneaking rotten eggs into shoes, stuffing balloons under seat cushions, even swapping ice cream with mustard (that one was brutal!). And since we looked almost identical back then, we once pulled the ultimate prank on our relatives: I chopped my hair short to match his, we dressed in the same clothes, and then stood in different rooms of the house. Our poor guests were convinced they were seeing double, and we laughed ourselves silly.

Book chat

When you saw the cover, what did you think this book would be about?

Have you read a book like this before?

Who was your favourite character and why?

What part of the book did you find the funniest?

Have you ever pranked anyone or been pranked?

If you had to think up a new title for the book, what would it be?

If you could ask any character in this book a question, who would you choose and what would you ask?

Who would you recommend this book to and why?

Book challenge:

Come up with your very own prank and jot down the steps.

Collins BIG CAT

Published by Collins
An imprint of HarperCollins*Publishers*

The News Building
1 London Bridge Street
London
SE1 9GF
UK

Macken House
39/40 Mayor Street Upper
Dublin 1
D01 C9W8
Ireland

Text © Henry White 2025
Design and illustrations © HarperCollins*Publishers* Limited 2025

10 9 8 7 6 5 4 3 2 1

ISBN 978-0-00-876796-9

All rights reserved. No part of this publication may be reproduced, stored in a retrieval system, or transmitted in any form by any means, electronic, mechanical, photocopying, recording or otherwise, without the prior written permission of the Publisher or a licence permitting restricted copying in the United Kingdom issued by the Copyright Licensing Agency Ltd, 5th Floor, Shackleton House, 4 Battle Bridge Lane, London SE1 2HX.

Without limiting the exclusive rights of any author, contributor or the publisher of this publication, any unauthorised use of this publication to train generative artificial intelligence (AI) technologies is expressly prohibited. HarperCollins also exercise their rights under Article 4(3) of the Digital Single Market Directive 2019/790 and expressly reserve this publication from the text and data mining exception.

British Library Cataloguing-in-Publication Data
A catalogue record for this publication is available from the British Library.

Download the teaching notes and word cards to accompany this book at:
http://littlewandle.org.uk/signupfluency/

Get the latest Collins Big Cat news at
collins.co.uk/collinsbigcat

Author: Henry White
Illustrator: Mai Ngo (Illo Agency)
Publisher: Laura White
Product manager and
    commissioning editor: Caroline Green
Series editor: Charlotte Raby
Development editor: Catherine Baker
Project manager: Emily Hooton
Copyeditor: Sally Byford
Proofreader: Catherine Dakin
Cover designer: Sarah Finan
Typesetter: 2Hoots Publishing Services Ltd
Production controller: Sophie Waeland

Printed in the UK.

MIX
Paper | Supporting responsible forestry
FSC™ C007454

This book contains FSC™ certified paper and other controlled sources to ensure responsible forest management.

For more information visit: www.harpercollins.co.uk/green

Made with responsibly sourced paper and vegetable ink

Scan to see how we are reducing our environmental impact.